Lynne's Last Christmas

A Battle with Dementia

By Donald Hricik

This book is dedicated to all those who have cared for loved ones with dementia.

Proceeds from sales of this book will be donated to the Alzheimer's Foundation of America and to University Hospitals Hospice of Northeast Ohio.

Kindle Direct Publishing December 2018

Epilogue published with permission of Father Tom Fanta.

Front Cover: Happier times; Lynne's first high tea, London, England October 28, 2012.

PROLOGUE

As I mention in the final chapter of this short book, I wrote most of it within a few weeks of my wife's death. Although I shared the original draft with my children (who corrected some details of my memories!), I intentionally put it away for almost seven months before re-reading it, adding several passages, and deciding whether recounting the last few years of Lynne's life would provide either pain or solace. It has provided both for me. My kids cried reading the final draft but, in sharing thoughts about the manuscript, we brought back memories of both the bad times and the good times we encountered during Lynne's life. I think the entire project was therapeutic for each of us. I'm not sure if the story will be relevant or of interest to anyone other than the closest of family members or friends. After all, most people have dealt with the death of a loved one – so we all have our own stories and memories. However, I truly hope that my own memories will provide comfort to the many other families who have cared for loved ones with this awful thing called *dementia.* You are not alone. *DH*

Chapter 1

December 25, 2017

Lynne's last Christmas was pretty crummy. It was December 2017. My adult children – Brian, Kevin, Lauren, and Michael – were all home for the holidays and wanted me to take Lynne in to the hospital on Christmas Day. Their mother was sick and getting sicker with each passing day. I begged them to wait until the next day. I knew this would be Lynne's last Christmas.

Christmas was crummy in part because Lynne would traditionally orchestrate most of the gift buying for me, the kids, nieces and nephews, and our granddaughter, Brielle. However, she was no longer able to drive a car and for that matter, could barely walk. We each tried to do our part to replace her role as the Christmas organizer, but did a lousy job - so everyone ended up with crappy presents. I took the easy way out and just gave the kids money.

Then there was the problem of what to get *Lynne* for Christmas. She had already become bedbound or chair bound and her every-day clothing was now limited to a few old tops, incontinence panties or diapers, and loose fitting pants or pajama bottoms. She no longer wore jewelry. In fact, she permanently took off her wedding rings because, as a consequence of her weight loss, her fingers had become too thin to support them. Our bedroom contained a pile of new clothes that Lynne had accumulated from birthdays, anniversaries, and holidays over the past two to three years – outfits that were never worn even once. The tags were still attached to many of them. So, clothes and jewelry were out of the question as Christmas gifts for Lynne this year. Her eyesight had deteriorated and she could no longer read – not even the romance novels that she was once passionate about. So, books or other reading materials weren't good ideas either.

We went through the Christmas morning ritual in what we had come to call our *new* family room (part of an addition that we put on the house in 2001). It's a room with a high ceiling where we put up our artificial fourteen-foot Christmas tree each year. I grew up hating the idea of artificial Christmas trees, but this one appeared majestic, fit the space of the new family room perfectly, and was something that the entire family came to love. It was the same Christmas morning routine – I played Santa Claus, distributing the gifts so each person got their fair share to open. We turned on a little background Christmas music – Andy Williams, Johnny Mathis, Frank Sinatra, Burl Ives – but our emotions were subdued. My kids and I were all wondering the same thing – if we take Mom in to the hospital tomorrow, will she ever return home? We were dealing with her dementia for more than two years but we all recognized that her health was now in serious jeopardy.

Lynne got three pairs of slippers and two pairs of gloves for her last Christmas. She never wore any of them.

Chapter 2

Some Things About Lynne

Before describing her illness and her last days in greater detail, there are a few things I'd like to share about my wife.

1. She loved parties, especially big ones with lots of people.
2. Most people loved interacting with her because she had a knack for focusing the conversation, not on herself, but on the person she was talking to – something that always made the person feel better about themselves.
3. She had an amazing ability to deal with people in trouble – e.g., friends or family members with depression or other emotional issues, or friends of my kids who had issues with alcohol or drugs. She was never judgmental, only caring and nurturing.
4. She was a consummate caregiver – she frequently housed family members or friends recovering from surgery or other illnesses. Her caregiving skills were not nursing skills but human skills with which she was able to comfort sick people – feeding, dressing, bathing, and mostly just talking to them.
5. She was very religious and remained a devout Catholic until she was physically unable to make it to Church.
6. Her hope and faith were most obvious over a five-year period when our son, Kevin, developed acute myelogenous leukemia at the age of eleven. He was initially in the hospital for almost eight months, went into remission after a bone marrow transplant (my daughter Lauren was the donor), relapsed four years later, and then went into a sustained remission that has now lasted twenty-four years. During many points in his illness I gave up hope and told Lynne that our son was about to die. She strongly resisted all of that negativity and used her faith in God to pull the entire family through the ordeal. Family and friends continue to remember this experience and how Lynne pulled us through it. A parish priest, Father Tom Fanta, befriended

Lynne, Kevin and our entire family during that dark time and ultimately referred to Kevin as Lynne's "miracle child". We were sad when Father Tom moved to a new parish on the other side of town.

7. She loved to drink wine (mostly white) and smoke cigarettes (yes, I'm a physician and quit smoking myself almost thirty years earlier but, embarrassingly, could never convince Lynne to give up the habit). During the final days when we were providing comfort care only, I even let her drink wine in the morning – at least it was a source of calories. I did not let her smoke, however, not so much to upset her (which it did) but for fear that she would drop a cigarette and set the house on fire. She pretty much dropped everything she tried to handle during those last few months. I only learned after Lynne's death that at least two of my children snuck cigarettes into the house and let Lynne smoke while I was at work. I won't name them here but presume these kids will go straight to hell some day for this egregious sin!'

8. She loved to travel with me and I with her. We both agreed that travel was one of the highlights of our married life. In retrospect I feel very lucky that I had many opportunities to travel both nationally and internationally when Lynne and I were relatively young. We had several wonderful vacation trips with the kids – not just Orlando, but Sanibel Island, Washington DC, San Francisco, New York City, Toronto, and even Las Vegas when our youngest son turned twenty-one. Lynne was particularly fond of visiting foreign countries and interacting with people from different cultures. If I had promised her to see the world after I retired, we would never have traveled anywhere. Lynne passed away one month before my planned retirement date.

9. Her highest priority in life was the happiness of her husband, children, and grandchild. She was all about family.

Chapter 3

Early Events

My kids and I have frequently discussed how and when Lynne's cognitive skills first began to deteriorate.

Although she was still mentally intact at the time, I think Lynne's health began to decline about four and a half years earlier when she was fifty-nine and had a routine screening colonoscopy that revealed colon cancer. As she was waking up from the light anesthesia given for the procedure, she heard the colonoscopist tell me, "We'll need to wait for the biopsy results, but we found a mass in the right colon." As the she was showing me photographs of the growth, Lynne perked up and announced, "It's cancer."

From that moment on, Lynne always had tremendous guilt feelings. Her mother, who rarely sought medical care, died of advanced colon cancer in her late sixties. Once Lynne's colonic biopsies confirmed cancer, her gastroenterologist surmised that her mother's cancer had also probably started growing in her late fifties. As a physician-husband, I frequently reminded Lynne that children of parents with colon cancer should begin colon cancer screening (i.e. colonoscopies) at the age of forty. But like her mother, Lynne had developed a loathing for traditional medical care – something that always stupefied me as a doctor – and she repeatedly resisted having the procedure done.

Her guilt derived from the idea that her life may have been much different if she had the colonoscopy ten years earlier when that cancer was likely nothing more than a benign polyp. To the extent that her subsequent life affected the kids and me in so many negative ways, she felt guilty that postponing the colonoscopy ultimately took

9

its toll on her loved ones. Whenever anything negative happened to a member of the family, Lynne would quietly tell me, "It's all *my* fault" – even when nothing could be further from the truth.

It didn't help that the management of her colon cancer went horribly wrong. First, there was a false alarm about the possibility of metastatic disease. The routine CT scans performed for staging purposes showed a nodule in the liver and multiple smaller nodules in the base of each of her lungs. However, a PET scan using cancer-avid isotopes was negative, suggesting against metastatic cancer.

To be safe, the colorectal surgeon asked a colleague specializing in hepatobiliary surgery to scrub in on the ensuing surgery to examine the liver and to biopsy the liver nodule – which proved to be a benign fatty tumor or *lipoma*. The lung lesions were deemed to be old scars – not cancer. The resection of the colon itself was done laparoscopically – a procedure for which our surgeon had become internationally famous. He told us that we would be home in three days, that only a small section of the right colon would be removed, and that Lynne would be left with plenty of colon to sustain normal bowel function.

We were *not* home in three days. The day after the operation, the surgeon left for a week to attend an academic meeting in Australia. Lynne started vomiting the next day and continued to vomit six to ten times daily for the next few days. The covering surgical attending attributed all of this to an *ileus* – i.e. a temporary bowel paralysis that can occur whenever the intestines are manipulated surgically - although we were told in advance that an ileus is very unusual after laparoscopic colectomies. After a week, I expressed some concern about Lynne's lack of nutrition. She could tolerate nothing by mouth without vomiting and so her nutrition was limited to the small amount of glucose given to her via IV fluids. A nasogastric (NG) tube was placed to decompress her upper GI tract. The original surgeon returned from his trip and, after reviewing a series of abdominal x-rays performed during his week of absence, concluded that Lynne did *not* have a simple ileus. Instead, he decided that she had a mechanical small bowel obstruction. Something was partially blocking her small intestines. She would need more surgery – both to confirm the suspected diagnosis and, hopefully, to fix the problem.

The second operation was *not* laparoscopic but instead involved a full vertical incision performed for a typical exploratory laparotomy. The surgeon was correct. An adhesion or scar had become attached to one of the internal surgical staples resulting in a band of tissue that was blocking the small intestine. As the surgeon told me afterwards, Lynne's remaining intestines were so swollen with backed up fluid that he literally had to squeeze the small bowel in a backwards fashion until the fluid left her body via the NG tube – a total of fifteen liters (almost four gallons) of fluid. If he hadn't removed the fluid that way, the intestines would have been too swollen to allow him to close the surgical wound – and that would have necessitated a *third* operation.

Not surprisingly, Lynne *did* have a true ileus after this major manipulation of her intestines, and she was miserable for several days, unable to eat anything, and with an uncomfortable NG tube that continuously drained her stomach to keep it decompressed. At the three-week mark, I once again spoke to her physician team about the lack of nutrition. Lynne got her Bachelor's degree in dietetics and worked as a hospital staff dietician both in Boston and in Cleveland for almost eight years before deciding to become a full-time Mom. Although she had become a little rusty with some of the modern principles of postoperative nutrition, she still recognized that IV fluids alone for three weeks are not enough to prevent malnutrition. NG tube feedings were out of the question because she was still draining fluid from her stomach in the opposite direction. With the attending surgeon again out of town, the covering surgeon reluctantly agreed to start intravenous nutrition through a peripherally inserted central catheter or PICC line – sort of like a regular IV line that is inserted and advanced into a central vein in a manner that minimizes infection of the IV catheter from skin bacteria.

My daughter, Lauren, and I had both happened to be in the Lynne's hospital room when the PICC line nurse arrived to perform the procedure. She happily allowed us to stay in the room to observe the procedure that went smoothly until the nurse injected a final "flush" of the new line. I'll never forget Lynne sitting bolt upright, turning gray in color, and gasping out "I can't breathe, I can't breathe." A floor nurse quickly called a "Code White" and using a finger pulse-oximetry device found her oxygen saturation to be 70% (normal is usually greater than 90%), suggesting that her lungs weren't getting enough oxygen. Lynne then exhibited some facial distortion with her eyes deviated and fixed in the left lateral position for about ten seconds. Lauren and I, to this day, are convinced we witnessed a seizure. However, by the time the Code White team arrived, these symptoms were completely gone, her pulse-oximetry reading normalized, and the team concluded that she had a simple vasovagal (fainting) episode.

BS.

I was too exasperated to disagree. At that point in time, being in the hospital for three weeks greatly frustrated Lynne when she was promised three days. Had I pushed the seizure issue, it would have taken several more days to get a neurologic evaluation – head CT scan, MRI, possibly an EEG and maybe even a spinal tap. Lauren and I pretended that we were happy with the diagnosis of a vasovagal episode. If Lynne truly had a seizure, it could have resulted from the low oxygen level alone. But I remember wondering whether she might have had a small stroke or something else wrong with her brain.

As it turned out, her PICC line was never used! The next day, the NG drainage became minimal and she was able to tolerate a liquid diet. We were sent home with instructions to advance her diet as tolerated. I removed the PICC line myself because no one instructed us otherwise and it would eventually get infected if left unused in her arm. Although Lynne was very unhappy with her surgeons during this hospitalization, she *loved* the nursing staff and ancillary personnel. From my perspective, however, the discharge planning was a little sloppy – maybe because Lynne became so frustrated with the long hospital stay that her complaints became almost abusive. I'm sure at least some of the staff was happy to see her go.

Despite the long hospital stay, Lynne insisted that we tell none of her friends or family (not even her brother and sister) about her colon cancer or her surgery. This need for complete privacy had been the case throughout her life whenever she had a medical illness or required surgery of any kind. It was a weird kind of Irish vanity that I never understood (okay, she was only one quarter Irish, but still stubborn). She never wanted family or friends to see her as anything other than a pillar of strength and a picture of perfect health. She would maintain this attitude until the final few months of her life. It became impossible to keep her colon cancer a secret for very long as family members became suspicious when Lynne stopped answering calls. However, Lynne never stopped being angry at me for talking to others about *her* medical problems.

The entire ordeal with colon cancer – eliminating the first half of one of Lynne's cherished summers - markedly enhanced her dislike and mistrust of the medical system. I did convince her to attend an outpatient visit for follow-up with the surgeon. He told us that, pathologically, the removed cancer had "equivocal" margins – meaning that the pathologist was not one hundred percent convinced that the tumor had not spread beyond the wall of the colon. The surgeon recommended that we see an oncologist and consider chemotherapy "just to be sure."

Lynne refused to do either, and forever thereafter claimed that she was never told anything about equivocal margins, oncologists, or chemotherapy. *Was she losing her memory or just being stubborn?*

She did reluctantly agree to a follow-up colonoscopy two years later. Lynne really liked the female colonoscopist who, among other things, had her own bout with colon cancer for which she also needed surgery. Lynne's repeat study was "clean" and, in retrospect, I'm quite sure that her cancer was cured by the initial surgery – despite all of the complications and concerns about metastatic disease. If she had received chemotherapy, we would have never known whether it was effective or not. As it turns out, it was never needed.

The problem is that we were told Lynne would have normal bowel movements because only a 'small part' of the right side of her colon was to be removed. However, Lynne experienced loose stools of varying intensity virtually *every* day of her life following that surgery. Diarrhea and fecal incontinence would ultimately replace loose stools as a problem she faced for the entire last year of her life. It was disconcerting that, after the follow-up colonoscopy, the gastroenterologist told us that the amount of large intestine originally removed was closer to sixty percent of the entire colon (not exactly a small part). She also informed us that, during one of her two operations, the ileocecal valve had been removed. We hadn't been told that before. That's a natural valve located where the small intestine connects to the large intestine and normally slows the flow of liquid stool from one to the other. It also prevents backwards reflux from the colon to the small bowel and may thus prevent reflux of bacteria to naturally minimize the risk of infection. Without an ileocecal valve, the remaining small portion of the colon may have been overwhelmed with the liquid contents of the small intestine. The gastroenterologist made some dietary recommendations to help with Lynne's loose stools, but Lynne wasn't interested in changing her diet. Some short-lived efforts to follow the gastroenterologist's recommendations never really helped anyhow.

It was around this time – or perhaps a year or two earlier that Lynne started losing her hair. Hair loss or *alopecia* is sometimes a sign of an underlying disease but not typically a sign of cancer or dementia. Furthermore, the hair loss was not the typical "male pattern" baldness that can be seen in women with thyroid disorders or systemic lupus erythematosus. Lynne's hair loss primarily involved the *back* of her head. As Lynne had a nervous habit of picking at her scalp, my children and I half-jokingly wondered whether she was literally pulling her hair out. Of course Lynne denied that. I never received any reasonable explanation for the hair loss from medical professionals. Looking back, it almost certainly had nothing to do with her underlying medical and neurological issues. However, as time went on and she began to lose weight, her thin body habitus combined with the loss of hair made her look almost skeletal.

I believe that Lynne was still thinking clearly back then but her constant guilt feelings and daily diarrhea formed a platform for the ensuing dementia that made her life miserable.

Chapter 4

Weight Loss

Even as a younger healthy woman, Lynne always had an active gastro-colic reflex, i.e., if she ate a meal, ~~should~~ she would need to move her bowels within thirty minutes. That's not too unusual – most human beings have at least a mild form of this normal reflex, which is Nature's way of keeping the GI tract moving along. Following her partial colectomy, Lynne's gastro-colic reflex became exaggerated. She would sometimes excuse herself from the dinner table to run to the bathroom. Early on, there were occasional minor accidents – mostly just some soiled underwear.

Eventually, Lynne became reluctant to attend social events when food was being served – too embarrassed to be running off to the bathroom or – God forbid – having an accident at the table. I'm not entirely sure, but I think all of this was the reason why her food intake gradually diminished. She would regularly fill up her plate with food, then play with it by pushing pieces back and forth across the plate, ultimately consuming very little. Every now and then when she did try to eat, she would experience nausea and vomit into a napkin, again feeling embarrassed when she was with family or friends. She increasingly hid food from her plate – rolling up pieces of food into a paper napkin or even in her clothing – to give us the impression that she was eating more than she really was. We all learned how to do that as young kids to fool our parents, but it wasn't normal adult behavior

Lynne was a strict practicing Catholic, but she stopped going to Mass on Sundays and Catholic holidays about two years before her death. My children and I had stopped going to church regularly many years earlier – for different and varied reasons, but we were stunned when Mom stopped going to church. I never really discussed this with Lynne. I believe she maintained her faith in God till the end and she certainly requested a Catholic burial, but with as much as she had been through in her life, it would be easy for me to understand how she might lose that faith. Now

I'm quite sure she stopped going to church, not because of any loss of faith, but because she was afraid of having an accident in the middle of Mass.

Her constant diarrhea and poor eating led to weight loss that actually predated any early signs of dementia. Again, I think these things were all connected. In her late forties and early fifties, Lynne had embarked on an exercise program – possibly motivated by me and my children who had been passionate about exercising and staying fit. She joined a local fitness center. Her exercise consisted almost exclusively of power walking on treadmills. She befriended some older and retired men who became treadmill buddies. I always joked about them hitting on her, and I'm sure that wasn't too far from the truth. Prior to starting her exercise program, Lynne weighed about 135 pounds and, at 5 feet 8 inches tall, already appeared attractively thin to me. With hard work she got her weight down to 125 pounds. At around the age of fifty, she was in the best shape of her life. I remember her in the bedroom proudly showing off her newly thinned waistline. When she was last able to stand on a scale for me – about six months before she died – she weighed 96 pounds. I'm sure she was closer to 80 pounds when she passed away. She had become cachectic in appearance – that is, looking like someone dying from cancer. Yet it happened so gradually that even family members sometimes couldn't appreciate how emaciated she had become.

Chapter 5

Memory Loss

The first signs of true cognitive impairment started two to three years before Lynne died - maybe late 2015 or early 2016. Memory loss would soon become evident, but it was preceded by repetitiveness. Lynne's mother, although never truly demented in my opinion, shared this tendency to repeat things. She would tell a story and, when finished, tell the entire story a second time – almost word for word – until the listener was inclined to say, "Yes, you already said that." It was irritating. When Lynne started this habit, I felt it must be an inherited trait but never thought of it as a first sign of serious dementia. Hey, we all get a little repetitive as we get older, right?

True memory loss followed shortly thereafter. It was almost exclusively short-term memory loss at first. Forgetting what she just said formed the substrate for her repetitiveness. But then she would forget key ingredients in meals she was preparing. She would forget what she had done earlier in the day. She forgot where she put things. She would forget how many people were coming to dinner and often set the wrong number dinner places. For years since the death of our own parents, Lynne and I would host Thanksgiving for about twenty family members at least every other year. By Thanksgiving of 2016 it became obvious to our extended family members that Lynne had lost her ability to organize a dinner party or to cook for such a big gathering. We all chipped in to help her out but that turned out to be the last time we would allow Lynne to plan a big family event – against her vigorous objections. She denied having any mental problems. She was always such an excellent cook. It was painful to see her lose those talents. It was just the beginning of a lot of pain.

Chapter 6

Falling

A couple of months before Thanksgiving of 2016, I took Lynne to Las Vegas – a place we both loved to visit. We loved the eating, drinking, gambling and the shows. And like most times when we traveled anywhere, there was almost always a little romance – but especially in Vegas. On our first morning of this particular trip – after arriving late the night before, I woke up early despite desperately trying to sleep in while Lynne was sitting in the corner of the hotel room, smoking a cigarette. I think *she* loved Vegas in part because it was one of the few places left in the US where hotels were allowed to have smoking floors and rooms.

I was already upset that Lynne had no interest in gambling the night before. When I woke up to complain about the smoke in the room, I noticed Lynne wearing a makeshift bandage – made of facial tissues and toilet paper - on her left lower leg. It was covered with dried blood. When I asked her what happened she told me she "nicked" her leg on the corner of the bed frame when she got up at night to go to the bathroom without the benefit of a night light. It seemed plausible. I got up, and removed the toilet paper bandage. Lynne had split open an eight-inch wound on the anterior aspect of her left lower leg – exposing the underlying fat and muscle. Had I been awake at the time of the original injury I would have taken her to an emergency room for stitches, but the wound looked to be at least eight hours old and the edges of the wound were mostly matted together. I went down to the gift shop and bought some medical gauze, returned to clean up the dried blood, tried my best to align the edges of the wound, and fashioned a more durable bandage of gauze and tape, hoping that the gash would heal without breaking down and getting infected. Lynne brought mostly short sundresses for the trip and was reluctant to leave the room because of the appearance of her leg. The leg was painful, so "romance" was out of the question. I ordered some bottles of wine for the room and we spent two days and nights in Vegas drinking wine and watching movies on TV.

Hey, 'what happens in Vegas stays in'...oh well. It was the first time we ever went to Vegas and returned home with almost as much money as we brought along for the trip – because we never spent a penny on gambling. It was our last time together to Sin City.

After that trip, it became obvious that Lynne's gait was disturbed. It was wide based – like you see in patients with cerebellar atrophy, but also "shuffling" – like she couldn't pick her feet up off the ground – a disturbance more reminiscent of Parkinson's Disease or normal pressure hydrocephalus. Around the same time she showed signs of psychomotor retardation – i.e., her thought processes and her physical movements became noticeably slower. This is also typical of Parkinson's Disease and I thought I had made a diagnosis – but she never developed the resting tremor that is classic for that disease and it was later dismissed by her neurologists.

Whatever the cause of her gait disturbance, falling became routine and Lynne sustained multiple injuries to her arms and legs during the next year. One night when I was working late, my sons, Brian took Lynne to one of our favorite local pubs for a light dinner of burgers and fries. According to Brian, in the middle of downing their meals, Lynne suddenly fell out of her chair on to the floor in front of the restaurant's manager and a number of shocked customers. Brian carefully picked Lynne up and brought her back home. When I asked her about the incident she told me that she just had a "dizzy spell". Dizziness became a rather common symptom that preceded many of her subsequent falls.

Fortunately, most of her falls were associated only with minor lacerations and shallow abrasions. Lots of blood, but no serious injuries. However, the lacerations on her extremities started adding up, and for the remainder of her life she had multiple wounds in various stages of healing on both arms and both legs. She never broke any bones or seriously hit her head although she did fall flat on her face in our bedroom one night and I awoke to find her laying on the floor with her head surrounded by a pool of blood. I feared that she might have bled into or around her brain but she was moving all of her extremities and seemed not to have any new neurologic deficits. You know, I scrubbed those blood stains with various detergents and stain removers for weeks and could not completely remove them. An outsider might not notice them now because they have finally faded a bit, but I can still see the stains to this day. They are awful reminders of an awful time. The next day Lynne had a black eye and a very black and blue nose. Any newcomer to our situation would probably suspect that I was physically abusing her.

I had an old walker in the garage left over from years earlier when I was recovering from back surgery. I dusted it off and encouraged Lynne to use it – at least for her nighttime trips from the bed to our master bathroom. At first, she adamantly refused to use the walker - but that changed with time. For many months she would wake me up in the middle of the night – at my insistence - to escort her to the bathroom – with or without the walker. Without my help, she would have fallen every time. Eventually she became dependent on the walker, not just for bathroom trips, but also for ambulation anywhere in the house. Obviously, there was no way I could be away from home at night and I ended up canceling a number of meetings and talks that normally filled my schedule and required travel out of town. I received invitations to give talks or to attend advisory board meetings in Rio de Janeiro, Brazil and in Edinburgh, Scotland. I was hoping that Lynne would be in good enough shape to join me on trips to these wonderful cities, but I was forced to cancel both trips because of her condition. Our international travels together had come to an end.

Chapter 7

Neuropsychiatric Evaluation

In November 2016, I convinced Lynne to see a neurologist from my hospital who was an expert in dementias. He was actually board certified in both in Neurology and Psychiatry. That seemed perfect because, at that point in time, many family members and friends had been questioning whether Lynne was just severely depressed (something that she vehemently denied until the end). I literally had to drag her to the appointment. When we first met the doctor in the waiting room of his office Lynne immediately pointed out (loudly in front of several other patients) 1) that she was there against her will (causing all the other waiting patients to stare at me with consternation), 2) that this was a one-time only visit, and 3) that she did not want me in the room as she was being examined. Not a great way to start a doctor-patient relationship.

The "examination" was really more of a mental status evaluation – lasting almost two hours. At the end of that evaluation, the neurologist convinced Lynne to allow me in the room. She was not happy with this and had a growl on her face when I walked in. The doctor's conclusions were that Lynne had significant short-term memory loss, that she had early signs of dementia, but that he did not have a specific diagnosis. I liked him a lot, and especially liked the way he dealt with a difficult patient like Lynne, but after a three-hour office visit, my initial response was, "Really? Tell me something I don't know!"

I noticed that the neurologist carefully avoided the term Alzheimer's Disease in postulating a diagnosis for Lynne's dementia. To some extent, I already knew that Alzheimer's Disease can only be diagnosed with histologic examination of brain tissue that could be obtained from a brain biopsy but more often as part of an autopsy (Lynne had neither of these). The term is often used by laypersons as a synonym for other forms 'dementia', but it is not the correct diagnosis in a large number of patients.

The neurologist wrote orders for some blood tests, an MRI of the brain, and a follow-up appointment in two months. Lynne refused to follow any of these recommendations.

Chapter 8

Summer of Tough Love

My house was literally a shitty mess from June to September of 2017. All of my kids were grown and gone, so Lynne and I were in an empty nest. However, the local children (Brian, Lauren, and Michael) visited often – eventually almost every day of the week. Kevin lived in Chicago but stepped up his visits to Cleveland to help out as much as he could. I can't put into words how helpful my children were and how much I *depended* on their help to get through the next year.

For Lynne, that summer was characterized by continued weight loss, increasing disorientation and confusion, progressive weakness such that she could barely ambulate – even with a walker, and multiple falls associated with more minor injuries. It was never clear to me whether Lynne developed true urinary and fecal incontinence. I think probably she was just too weak to get to a bathroom. One way or another, she began wetting and soiling herself regularly. Lauren and Kevin had formerly worked as medical assistants at my hospital and were familiar with the work involved with "total care" patients – i.e., bedbound, confused and incontinent patients who were almost always pre-terminal. This came in handy in caring for Lynne, but I'm sure it felt completely different taking care of a "total" when that person happened to be their mother. Brian was less comfortable dealing with bed and diaper changes but helped in so many other ways. Eventually, he did much of his banking work while stationed in my home, so that – between conference calls and computer work, he was available for long periods of time to help with meals, to help spell me and his siblings, and most importantly, to spend time talking with his mother and keeping her company. Michael, the youngest of the clan, was somewhere in between. He also worked as a data analyst in my hospital and had some exposure to sick patients but had no direct experience with their day-to-day care. Yet, not infrequently, he helped us with his mother's nursing care – reminding me often that "It's a dirty job, but somebody has to do it."

By mid-summer we were regularly dressing Lynne in incontinence underwear but these did not completely prevent major accidents that resulted in wetting or soiling the family room couch. Lynne always had her favorite sitting position on that couch in the *old* family room. There was a divot the shape of her bony butt there to prove it. To avoid destruction of many pieces of furniture, I insisted that she occupy *only* that spot during the daytime. She would have as many as four bowel movements per day. As the summer progressed, all of her bowel movements took the form of nasty liquid diarrhea. I became a major investor in baby wet wipes. When she soiled one couch cushion to the point that it was cruel punishment to let her sit in her own excrement, I would replace it with another cushion from the same couch, then manually wash the soiled cushion, hanging it outside to air dry. I bought a one-year supply of Febreeze. It was a useless effort after a few runs. The couch and the entire old family room smelled like an outhouse and it became embarrassing to let anyone into our home.

Our master bedroom is on the second floor of the house. By late summer I literally had to carry Lynne up the stairs to bed – or at least assisted her one painful step at a time after which we were both thoroughly exhausted. Many times, she would literally crawl up those stairs, taking twenty to thirty minutes to get to the second floor.

It was during the summer of 2017 that Lynne stopped bathing. Our full bathrooms were both on the second floor, so just getting to one of them was part of the problem. Ten years earlier, we remodeled our master bedroom that previously had a walk-in shower but no bathtub. Lynne loved to take an occasional bubble bath and so, without compromising the overall space we scrapped the shower and re-configured the bathroom to include a tub with its own showerhead. However, even when I could get Lynne to the second floor, she could not coordinate her legs to step over the side of the tub into the bath water and she became morbidly afraid of slipping and falling. I so wished that we hadn't gotten rid of that walk-in shower! The kids' bathroom down the hall had a shallower tub. A month earlier, Lauren had modest success in using this tub to bathe her mother. At a time when Lynne was still ambulating with a walker, I took her to that bathroom, filled the tub, undressed her, and literally lifted her and placed her in the water. I helped her wash her body and also washed her hair, keeping a steady flow of warm water in the tub, and occasionally opening the drain to eliminate the grime that came off her body. It was strangely sensual and reminded me of earlier, happier times during our marriage. It probably had been three months since her last bath or shower and the look on Lynne's face was one of ecstasy.

That was the good news. The bad news was that I hadn't anticipated the ordeal of getting Lynne *out* of the tub. The bathtub had sliding doors – I guess designed for privacy. But those doors made the extraction from the tub even more awkward and difficult. With my first attempts to grab Lynne's arms and bring her to her feet, her legs gave out and she slipped back into the water several times. With each grab of her arms I could feel her tissue paper-like skin ripping to cause new lacerations or bruises. I was indeed physically abusing her but only with good intentions. I then decided to empty the tub. Now Lynne was uncomfortably shivering and still slipped on the slick bottom surface of the tub. I finally stripped down to my underwear, got into the tub with her and again literally lifted her to a position where she was sitting precariously on the edge of the tub. I squeezed by her, being careful not to let her slip in either direction, and gently lowered her naked and emaciated body to the bathroom floor. Before covering her with towels, Lynne looked at me. I was literally sweating and breathing rapidly from the effort. Then she looked down at herself and said, "Look what I've done to myself. Look at what I've done to you." It was that pervasive feeling of guilt. She felt as though she was to blame for everything.

It was Lynne's last time in a bathtub. We did our best to keep her clean with sponge baths whenever we could. Lauren would also use a pot of hot water and wash her hair every now and then.

My children started insisting that I "intervene" by forcing Lynne to be hospitalized – but she strongly resisted and so did I, initially. One Sunday in August, after a family dinner to celebrate Brian's birthday, Lynne was attempting to get up from her couch seat and fell to the hardwood floor, right in front of me and the kid, lacerating her leg. Without any hesitation, my daughter called 911 and the local EMS squad arrived five minutes later. We were all thinking – 'this is it - now she will *have* to be hospitalized for evaluation and treatment'. Lynne screamed in anger when the EMS team arrived. At one point I held her arms forcefully to calm her down from her agitated state and opened a new laceration on her left arm. The guys from EMS were very nice and very professional. However, Lynne refused to cooperate. She even refused to allow them to take her vital signs. It was an ugly scene. When she properly identified the correct time, place, and persons in the room – the EMS squad concluded that she was fully oriented and competent. Under those circumstances they could not force her into their ambulance or to go to any hospital. When I pointed out that she was at risk for falling and sustaining a head injury or broken bones, they could only respond, "Call us back if that happens." My kids and I were incredibly frustrated. Lynne may have gotten the right time, place and person, but we knew that she was no longer competent.

About a month later, one of my children (I only later learned that it was Lauren) called the County Protective Service Department and reported that a woman living at my address was at risk of harming herself. A County worker called me to report this and arranged an elective meeting with me and Lynne to investigate. Although I had prepared Lynne for this visit she seemed totally surprised when the worker arrived and initially asked me to send her away. She acquiesced but then belittled all of her problems and convinced the worker that she was getting better, falling less, eating well – and that she had no need for hospitalization.

The worker was astounded that Lynne was still driving and, based on her recommendation, I hid Lynne's car keys. Indeed, my kids had received calls from our local bank and from Lynne's beauty shop to express alarm that we were still allowing Lynne to drive to these establishments as she appeared barely able to stand up straight, let alone to walk or drive. To say the least, Lynne was not happy about losing her car keys and driving privileges, and I endured countless rants but never gave in. She punished me by making me the person in charge of buying her cigarettes. Two packs at a time, two or three times a week. I hadn't realized that cigarettes were now costing almost nine dollars a pack! The Indian guy behind the counter at the local convenient store recognized me well after a while and had "my order" ready to go before I even opened the door to his store.

Among other things, Lynne's inability to drive meant that as of September 2017, I was responsible for all of the grocery shopping which I heretofore had *very* little experience with. Lynne got a manicure done once a week and, to maintain some semblance of normalcy, I started taking Friday mornings off from work to take her to the beauty shop. The gals at the shop loved Lynne but I could tell by their behavior that they knew there was something seriously wrong with one of their favorite clients.

The County worker's second visit – about two weeks later – was unannounced. When she found out that Lynne had suffered from multiple additional falls during the interim period – she threatened Lynne with "institutional commitment" unless she agreed to be hospitalized.

Lynne took the threat seriously – especially when the worker described the institution as "more like a prison than a hospital". She reluctantly agreed to be admitted to my hospital for an evaluation. On the morning that I drove her to the hospital I noticed that she was crying as she looked back at our house. It reminded me of our mutual emotions when we moved away from our first house years earlier.

It is sad to permanently leave a place that you have come to know and love. On this occasion, there were no words spoken between us but I could tell from the look on Lynne's face that she was thinking 'I'll never see my home again'. I think she was concerned that she would be hospitalized for the rest of her life, or perhaps left to die in a prison-like nursing home. She was wrong, of course, but as she became increasingly disoriented during the next nine months, I don't think she remained fully cognizant of those physical and intangible things that had made our house the *home* that it had become over thirty years.

Because she had no primary care physician, I arranged an admission to our Hospitalist Service with planned consultations from Neurology and Gastroenterology. I honestly was very concerned about the possibility that Lynne's colon cancer had returned – maybe even with metastases to the brain. However, a brain CT scan showed no structural lesions that would have suggested cancer or a stroke. CT scans of her abdomen and pelvis showed no evidence of recurrent or metastatic cancer. About ten months after it was initially recommended, a brain MRI was finally performed and showed severe diffuse cerebral atrophy – a term indicating shrinkage of all components of the brain. The neurologist commented that, at the age of sixty-four, Lynne's brain size appeared to be that of a ninety-five year old woman.

My daughter and I were in the room when the neurologist performed a formal mental status examination. We were both stunned by Lynne's diminished memory and cognitive skills. She could not draw a clock or the hands of a clock within the amount of specified time. She was asked to count backwards from the number 100, serially subtracting 7 from the previous number. Her first number was 92 and the second was 78 – and that was as far as she could go. She was asked to remember five words and ten minutes later could only recall two of the five. Gastroenterology reviewed the CT scans and thought there were signs of inflammation in the area of the remaining colon. Since her predominant problem was neurological, they suggested only that we schedule another outpatient colonoscopy electively. I knew that Lynne would refuse to cooperate with *that* recommendation.

She was sent home with some new medications. Neurology recommended memantine for dementia, mirtazapine for possible depression and appetite stimulation, and medicinal marijuana to stimulate appetite and prevent nausea. GI recommended only loperamide (i.e. Imodium) for her diarrhea.

Chapter 9

Social Isolation

Lynne had always been the life of most parties. When it came to neighborhood parties, I would often head home before 10 pm but Lynne would usually stay until the early morning hours, drinking, smoking and chatting with her close friends. The same was definitely true when we threw our own parties. Lynne loved *big* parties with lots of people. We have an in-ground pool in our backyard and she particularly loved big summer pool parties. In the fall she enjoyed hosting clambakes to which she invited the entire neighborhood. Everyone loved Lynne's food and there was never any shortage of beer, wine, and booze.

All this made it particularly painful to witness Lynne's gradual withdrawal from social interactions. In the late summer of 2016, we went to a wedding reception for one of our neighbor's daughters. It was held at an old renovated warehouse in downtown Cleveland. You took an elevator to get to one of four floors in the place. The cocktail hour took place on the outdoor rooftop of the warehouse. About fifteen minutes into the party, a friend walked up to me and asked where Lynne was. I figured she was just chatting with other friends out of view. After thirty minutes I could not spot her and wandered around the rooftop looking for her with no luck. I thought maybe she just went out for a smoke. After forty-five minutes, with dinner about to begin, I got nervous and took the elevator down to the ground floor and out to the parking lot where I found Lynne wandering somewhat aimlessly. She had no more than a half a glass of wine before getting lost so I knew she wasn't drunk (in fact, despite her fondness for wine, I rarely if ever saw Lynne intoxicated during our marriage). She told me that she just needed some fresh air (weird because the cocktail party was *outdoors*) and that she then couldn't find the elevator (which was eminently visible as you entered the building). During the dinner, she was unusually quiet and told me she didn't care for the food and so basically had nothing to eat.

In the spring of 2017, we attended our niece's wedding at a downtown hotel. Lynne again ate none of the food, interacted minimally with the new bride and groom or other family members, and asked me to take her home before 9 pm. I believe this was the last time that Lynne and I attempted to have dinner together at an outside venue. Previously we loved going out to eat – whether it was a local pub or fine dining at elegant restaurants, especially when traveling either in the US or abroad. I will always miss sharing excellent food at fine restaurants with my wife.

That summer, we *did* attend a backyard "going away" party for a couple that had been friends and neighbors for more than two decades. They were downsizing and moving to a different suburb. Lynne wore pants that exposed many of the wounds on her lower legs. I was surprised because she previously had worn clothes designed to hide the wounds. Although she didn't eat much if anything, I recall that she interacted reasonably well with many of the neighbors who attended this party. Months later, some of these neighbors told me that it was the first time they noticed that Lynne "wasn't right". Again, I'm willing to bet that some neighbors worried about physical abuse when they saw the wounds on Lynne's arms and legs and first noticed her depressed affect.

The last dinner with extended family occurred on Thanksgiving of 2017. It was a lovely affair that my niece and her husband hosted. Lynne was initially devastated that *she* would not be hosting Thanksgiving as she had so many times before – but ultimately understood why we were changing the tradition. We had some pleasant conversations prior to dinner and Lynne actually ate a few morsels of the Thanksgiving feast, but then became rather quiet and asked me to take her home before the pumpkin pies were served. For many of my close family members, that was the last time they would see Lynne before she entered hospice care. When we arrived home she headed directly for the bathroom, making me think that our early departure from Thanksgiving dinner was partly related to her bowel issues. She then assumed her usual position on the couch, lit a cigarette and asked me for a glass of wine that she spilled just before falling asleep.

Chapter 10

Limbo Months

Between September and December of 2017, Lynne's condition transitioned from slight improvement to gradual deterioration. Following her September admission, she agreed to a follow-up office visit with the original neurologist although we never saw him – only his nurse practitioner. The cognitive tests were repeated and showed some minor improvement. Perhaps the memantine was helping. I thought the marijuana actually lifted Lynne's spirits if not her appetite, but the neurologist felt that it was contraindicated in a demented patient. He was apparently angry with his hospital colleagues for prescribing it in the first place and, according to his nurse practitioner, refused to renew the prescription. When I pointed out that Lynne was still having diarrhea several times daily despite the loperamide, the neurology team could only recommend following through with the recommended outpatient colonoscopy.

Right.

Even before this hospitalization, but certainly for the ensuing few months, Lynne adamantly refused to allow non-nuclear family members, friends, or other guests to enter the house. I think she finally understood that she was sick and was embarrassed to admit it and to allow others to witness her condition. When the doorbell rang or someone knocked on the door, we were told not to answer. Lynne was still using her cell phone but refused to answer calls or text messages. She even refused to return phone calls from her beloved Father Tom who had been apprised of Lynne's deterioration by my children. She was angry that *anyone* would have the audacity to tell Father Tom that she was ill. My kids and I were also embarrassed to have visitors see our home in increasing disarray, so we were not completely opposed to the new rules. However, we faced a progressively worsening struggle dealing with friends and family members who sometimes seemed angry that we were not allowing them to see or communicate with Lynne. The truth is, we would have been very happy to get some outside help – or even some encouragement from outside visitors, but Lynne continually refused it.

Soiling her underwear and the couch became a daily routine – it wasn't a question of "if" but "when". She would regularly deny that she had soiled her pants and fought with me every time I tried to change her – making the entire process even more difficult than it already had to be.

By November, I was no longer able to assist Lynne up the stairs to her bedroom and left her to sleep on the old family room couch. On more than one occasion I was astounded to hear my bedroom door opening, finding that Lynne had crawled up the stairs to be with me. I would drag her up into our bed and cried myself to sleep – always hoping that I would not awaken in the morning in a pool of urine or diarrhea. When she did sleep on the family room couch, I would sleep poorly, constantly worrying that she would fall off the couch. Every noise in the house was Lynne falling to the floor until proven otherwise. I woke up several times each night running downstairs to make sure she was okay sleeping on the couch. The doctors prescribed nothing for sleep but I learned that over-the-counter Benadryl worked well. I gave her one to three of these at bedtime and had pretty good success in putting her to sleep. However, no matter how much I worried, how often I ran down the stairs, or how much Benadryl I gave Lynne, I woke up to find her laying on the floor next to the couch about once a week. In retrospect, I know this sounds almost criminal and if my kids had known how often I had allowed Lynne to fall off that couch they probably would have had *me* institutionalized for abandonment. At the time I thought I was doing my best. Even if I had chosen to sleep in the living room with Lynne, it probably wouldn't have prevented her from falling on the floor. And I'm not sure I could ever fall asleep with the stench in that room.

All of this eventually *did* become evident to my kids. By December they were ready for another intervention.

Chapter 11

December 26, 2017

Instead of arranging for an elective admission, we intentionally planned a morning visit to the Emergency Room – partly because I thought Lynne might require admission to the Intensive Care Unit. Her initial examination and lab studies all confirmed that she was severely dehydrated. Her urine was dark and foul smelling and she was started on broad-spectrum antibiotics for a suspected urine infection although the urine culture ultimately came back negative. She was started on IV fluids and a Foley catheter was inserted into her bladder to monitor her urine output.

The Neurology Service evaluated Lynne in the ER and thought that she had a new left-sided facial droop suggesting a stroke – but an urgent head CT scan was negative. The diagnosis of underlying dementia was already established so Neurology had little else to offer. She was admitted to a regular floor where the evaluation focused on her diarrhea, weight loss and poor oral intake. Under normal circumstances, a trial of tube feedings using a nasogastric tube would be warranted in a case like Lynne's, but I knew my wife and knew that in her confused state she would likely pull out an NG tube repeatedly. I also figured that she would need feedings for a prolonged period of time and so I convinced the GI Service to place a gastrostomy tube (i.e., a tube surgically placed into the stomach directly through the upper wall of the abdomen) so that feeding solutions could be administered immediately.

On the second hospital day, while I was at the hospital with Lynne, my three sons went to my house and removed the soiled couch from our old family room, putting it in our unheated back porch temporarily. With the porch door closed, we could once again breathe in the house without inhaling that smell of excrement. A few weeks later, I finally admitted that I would never be able to adequately clean the couch, so my sons carried it out to our tree lawn for the garbage department to pick up. I happened to be home the next morning for the garbage pick-up and laughed as I watched the workers reluctantly pick up the soiled couch to discard it, literally holding their noses. In the mean time, all of my children took responsibility for rearranging the furniture in my house to make up for the lost couch. Getting rid of that couch remains symbolically important to me. Essentially my own children were telling me "When we are dealing with something bad, we roll up our sleeves and take care of it." Indeed, that was pervasive attitude that characterized the family's subsequent approach to dealing with Lynne's illness.

During the first week in the hospital, the doctors and nurses had great difficulty maintaining venous access for fluids and medications. This was remarkable because Lynne always had "pipelines" for veins in her hands, arms and legs – but like the rest of her body, those veins had atrophied and all but disappeared. Lynne's overall discomfort was made even worse from the multiple efforts to puncture needles into invisible veins. She felt like a pincushion. It was easy to understand why she loathed the idea of being admitted to the hospital. One of the Hospitalists finally was able to insert a central IV catheter into her right external jugular vein, hoping that it could be used for several days.

To evaluate Lynne's severe diarrhea, the GI service appropriately wanted to perform the colonoscopy that had been recommended months earlier. Of course, performance of a colonoscopy requires a preparation to cleanse the colon, and that preparation, by definition, causes diarrhea – just what Lynne did *not* need. And of course, all food had to be held after midnight for the morning procedure – so Lynne missed about twelve hours of caloric intake to facilitate the colonoscopy. Despite getting half a gallon of the laxative solution, GoLytely, via her gastrostomy tube, the first attempt at the colonoscopy failed because there was too much stool in the rectum. That precludes a good look at the lining of the colon, which is necessary for the colonoscopist to see signs of inflammation or to detect polyps or tumors. Lynne was sent back to the floor for a second round of GoLytely and another night without tube feedings, and another day with more diarrhea. Lynne's exasperation was mounting. So was mine. The next morning, the Transport Service arrived to take her down for another attempt at the colonoscopy. While transferring her from the hospital bed to a cart, the transporter inadvertently trapped Lynne's IV tube around an IV pole, ripping the line out of her neck. Lynne screamed with pain as venous blood saturated her clothing and the bed sheets. Among other things, she realized that she would have to go through another round of venous sticks to re-establish vascular access for fluids and medications. She was not happy.

The second attempt at colonoscopy was aborted – again because of "inadequate preparation." I was astounded and frustrated. Lynne had received over a gallon of GoLytely in twenty-four hours and had consumed virtually no food. It seemed impossible that she had not been adequately "cleaned out". We had admitted her, in part, for evaluation of diarrhea, weight loss and malnutrition, and after four days in the hospital all of these problems were worse, not better.

Around this time, Father Tom Fanta paid a visit to Lynne. I was not present at the time but was told that her confusion, pain, and exasperation all melted away temporarily as she extended her arms to her old friend and confidant. He recognized the severity of Lynne's illness and, among other things, administered the Last Rites. Had it not been for Father Tom's visit and inspiration, it is quite possible that Lynne may have given up completely at that time. I'll forever be in debt for his friendship and his understanding of Lynne's life history and her unique persona.

The third attempt at colonoscopy revealed the underlying problem. The colonoscopist discovered a giant *fecolith* – i.e., a large hard-as-concrete ball of stool – stuck in the sigmoid colon – firmly attached to the wall of the intestine. She literally used a chisel like instrument to chip away at the fecolith and ultimately extracted it. All of this indicated that Lynne's problem was not *diarrhea* at all – it was severe *constipation* that resulted in a fecal impaction. In such cases, the colon literally forces liquid stool around the impaction with the final result being liquid bowel movements. And what had I been giving Lynne for months? Tons of loperamide – an anti-diarrheal agent that may well have contributed to the formation of the stool ball. I still wonder if that fecolith had been present for years. If Lynne didn't have chronically loose stools, would she have been more socially interactive? Would she have eaten better? Would she have maintained her weight and her strength? Would she have avoided the frequent falls and injuries? It is so easy to look back and wonder about these and other questions. Unfortunately, the damage had already been done.

In some ways, all of this was *good* news – at least we now understood the pathophysiology of Lynne's "diarrhea". Ironically, the recommended treatment was a laxative regimen to prevent constipation – so Lynne *continued* to have loose stools. Not surprisingly she developed severe anal irritation that even huge amounts of Preparation H did not help. Still, I was hopeful that we could proceed with aggressive tube feedings and that, despite Lynne's dementia, we could reverse her malnutrition, restore normal bowel function and get her home in reasonable shape. Because of my renewed hope, at this stage of the game I constantly reminded Lynne's medical team that she was a "full code". That meant that in the case of a catastrophic cardiac or respiratory arrest, we would want everything done to save her life including cardiopulmonary resuscitation (CPR), intubation (if she needed to be on a respirator), and transfer to an intensive care unit if needed.

Eleven days after admission, Lynne became acutely disoriented and started hallucinating – mostly visual hallucinations like seeing people and objects that were not really present in her hospital room. Some members of her medical team felt that her dementia was accelerating rapidly. But this was *not* dementia. It was *delirium* superimposed on her underlying dementia. Her Foley catheter was left in her bladder inexplicably for ten days and I suspected that she might be septic from a urine infection. I was right. She was started on antibiotics and her urine and blood cultures both came back positive. Her delirium improved over the next four or five days.

However, it was a *slow* improvement and during those few days, Lynne would continue to experience bouts of delirium sometimes associated with labored breathing. One night, I was sleeping alone at home, and was called at around midnight by one of the floor nurses at the hospital. She told me that Lynne looked bad and was having difficulty breathing and concluded that "We think you should get down here as soon as possible." I immediately presumed that Lynne was dead. From years in practice, I knew that, when people died in the hospital, it was customary to call relatives and ask them to come to the hospital without announcing the death for fear that they would become anxious, drive crazily to the hospital and cause a major accident. It was late at night and I didn't want to call my children and alarm them. I tearfully drove to the hospital expecting to hear the details of Lynne's last hours and mentally prepared myself for the subsequent tasks: informing the kids and other family members, making funeral arrangements, etc. When I got to the hospital floor, none of the nurses claimed to have called me. The shift change occurred long before midnight, so any nurse who called me at midnight would still have been working on the floor. I was told that Lynne *did* have a rough evening with some hallucinations but that she settled down and was now quite stable. To this day, I'm not sure if I had a hallucination of my own that night. I quickly visited Lynne who was sleeping calmly, kissed her on the forehead, returned home and slept soundly for the remainder of the night. I don't believe I told my kids about this episode until weeks or months later. I fell asleep thinking that maybe we still had a chance for recovery. I also hoped and prayed that it wasn't *me* going crazy.

The next major issue was Lynne's profound weakness. With all of the imaging studies, multiple colonoscopies and other tests – she was essentially bedbound save for one daily stint sitting in a chair. She was unable to ambulate and continued to soil her diapers. Physical Therapy was consulted, but Lynne typically refused their services – something that typically happened when I, the kids and I were not present

41

to protest. Her caregivers recommended transfer to the hospital's skilled nursing facility (SNF). The expectations were that she would get intense physical therapy in the SNF, that her strength would improve, and that she could be discharged home in one to two weeks.

After one week at the SNF, the Physical Therapy team met with me to discuss the difficulties they were having with Lynne. On at least three occasions I watched two therapists attempt to get Lynne to sit on the side of the bed and then to stand up. Each time Lynne screamed in pain and accused the therapists of trying to torture her. In our meeting the head therapist told me that Lynne was making no progress, that she no longer qualified for skilled nursing, and that our insurance company would likely threaten to stop paying for her inpatient care in the SNF within days.

A hospital Social Worker met with me to discuss two main options: transfer to a Nursing Home or discharge home with Hospice Care. Although Lynne's clinical status was bleak, the decision was easy. First of all, I was told that nursing homes would cost about $12,000 a month – and I had no long-term insurance to cover the cost that would have to come out of pocket. Hospice care was covered by my health insurance. Now, as a physician, I often equated the term "hospice" with terminal care – mostly for patients dying from cancer, but representatives from the hospital's hospice service assured me otherwise and that some patients remained in hospice care for months or years. They also explained that I could choose inpatient hospice care or home hospice care. Here there was really no choice. I had an immediate recollection of the tears in Lynne's eyes back in September when she thought she was leaving home forever. I would not let that happen. My kids and I wanted Lynne to come home.

Chapter 12

Hospice – First Two months

The idea was that Lynne would come home for comfort care measures only. We changed her status to DNR (do not resuscitate). The staff at the SNF told me that Lynne would be bed bound for the remainder of her life. We decided to leave the gastrostomy tube in place but also decided to *stop* the tube feedings. If she couldn't eat on her own, she would likely starve to death - a common mode of exit for patients with severe dementia. She was sent home on lorazepam (Ativan) for sedation, quetiapine (Seroquel) for anxiety and for sleep, and oral morphine sulfate as needed for pain or sedation.

A hospital bed was delivered to our home on the day Lynne was discharged. We rearranged our new family room to serve as her hospice bedroom and moved an old TV from one of my son's bedrooms and kept it running almost 24/7 to keep Lynne's mind occupied. My sons had already moved the couch from the *new* to the *old* family room when they threw out the old soiled couch, so this helped provide space for Lynne's bed and other hospital equipment and medical supplies. The hospital bed looked uncomfortable but the air mattress feature prevented decubitus ulcers (bed sores) and worked well for that purpose. She never once developed a bedsore. The guardrails of the hospital bed were not very tall, and we learned quickly that Lynne could easily crawl over the rails and fall out of bed. In fact, in the first month at home, she slept very poorly and surprised us all by sitting up regularly, swinging her legs over the guard rails, trying to stand up. She was supposed to be bedbound! We borrowed a cot from a neighbor and at night positioned it immediately next to Lynne's bed with the other side of her bed against a wall. We realized that someone would need to sleep on the cot every night and I took turns with my children. Lynne would still try to jump out of bed but would end up jumping on the lucky person sleeping next to her.

In my career as a physician, I had witnessed a lot of good nursing care – mostly in the inpatient hospital setting. However, the hospital's Hospice Service was truly *extraordinary.* One of the hospice nurses would visit at least twice weekly and more often if we had specific issues to address. In addition to taking vital signs and making an overall clinical assessment, the nurse changed the multiple bandages that covered the dozens of wounds on her extremities. The nurse would also keep track of Lynne's medicines and ordered refills that were delivered to the house promptly the same day. A hospice nursing aid would visit three to four times weekly and give Lynne sponge baths, assist us with diaper and clothing changes, freshen up her mouth and teeth, and wash her hair. Speaking of hair, during this otherwise unpleasant time, Lynne's chronic hair loss mysteriously resolved. Despite the monumental deterioration of the rest of her body, she had a full head of hair at the end of her life. It seems likely that she had been pulling her own hair out for years. Go figure.

A hospice Social Worker visited about once every two weeks. A music therapist dropped by a couple of times to play some soothing acoustic guitar tunes. A Catholic priest or Eucharistic minister came regularly to administer Holy Communion. All of these personnel were very professional and treated Lynne with incredible compassion. Just as importantly, they provided a great deal of family support recognizing how stressful the situation was for us.

However, the Hospice Service could spend only a limited amount of time in our home. I hired a Senior Care agency to provide "aids" anywhere between twelve and twenty hours per week. The aids were all quite nice but most had limited nursing skills and were more like babysitters. Lynne bonded with two or three of the aids that were assigned to her case most often. I will never be able to thank these people enough for their compassionate care of my wife. It was costing me almost $3000 a month, out of pocket, but certainly that was less than the cost of a full-time nursing home. My nearby sisters and Lynne's sister and brother were also very helpful in volunteering their time to sit with Lynne. Each of them had a calming effect on her that was much appreciated. For almost a year, Lynne had resisted having visitors – embarrassed by her condition and appearance. All that changed with time and Lynne was happy to allow friends and family members to visit and recount the good old days. She undoubtedly understood that some of these social calls would be the last time the visitors would see her alive.

When it became clear that Lynne was *not* bedbound, the Hospice Service ordered a Broda chair – which is kind of a Lazy Boy on wheels. This would allow her to sit up and watch TV or interact with family, but also allowed us to move her around the first floor of the house to give her more than just four walls to stare at. However, getting her up or down stairs was out of the question. Lynne would never see our master bedroom or our bed again for the remainder of her life.

We were all shocked to see that, within the first month, Lynne was *not* the bedbound hopeless case that Physical Therapy portrayed at the SNF. It was even more shocking that Lynne began to eat – liquids only at first but ultimately regular solid foods. At one point she was consuming more than a thousand calories per day.

Don't get me wrong. Her dementia was still severe and even worsening progressively. She always thought she was some place other than home. If I was sleeping on the cot next to her and she woke up before me, she would tap me on the shoulder, ask me to get her clothes and the car keys, and order me to take her "home". She never believed us when we told her she was already in her own home. She constantly demanded cigarettes although I refused to give in and allow her to smoke. Many times we caught her smoking imaginary cigarettes, carefully knocking off imaginary ashes into an imaginary ashtray. That was okay by me, and I was saving nine bucks a day!

Lauren had the brilliant idea of asking Lynne's manicurist at the beauty shop to make "house calls" to do Lynne's nails, as she was accustomed to on a weekly basis for years. The manicurist loved Lynne and was more than happy to comply and these turned out to be touching sessions, seeing my wife in her former glory.

Lynne became fond of calling out names of former family members and friends to come help her and to take her home. This included "Mom" and "Dad" – both deceased many years earlier - and "Judy" a childhood friend who also died tragically years ago in her forties. Reminding Lynne that these old friends were dead didn't help. She accused us of lying and insisted that all these people were alive and living in her room – ready to take her home. Interestingly, she rarely called my name or the names of my children when she wanted something – even though we were the ones with her about ninety percent of the time.

Now, during our otherwise crummy Christmas of 2017, fully aware that Lynne's condition would likely deteriorate thereafter, I offered my children one other gift. I would take them, two at a time (so the other two could stay home to care for Mom) on an all expenses paid long weekend trip to New York City. Lynne and I loved New York City but she would never again be in shape to travel. I made arrangements to take Brian and Michael to Manhattan in April. I knew in advance that the trip might need to be cancelled if Lynne was in bad shape at the time. However it turned out that she was relatively stable at the time and so we made the trip. Several months after Lynne's death, I separately took Lauren and Kevin to New York to complete my Christmas promise. The two boys and I stayed in midtown Manhattan and had a blast for three days and two nights, visiting the Memorial at Ground Zero, walking and shopping around Rockefeller Center, visiting St. Patrick's Cathedral, going to excellent (and expensive) restaurants, and doing our share of bar hopping. Kevin was back in Chicago at that time so it turns out that Lauren was mostly by herself with Lynne – although Lynne's sister, Cheryl, also stopped by each day to help. The text messages that Lauren sent to New York were all encouraging. Lynne was "eating like a horse" and seemed mentally clearer than she had been for weeks. It certainly made it more comfortable for my sons and I to be away for even a short little vacation. Lauren was appropriately proud that she had taken such good care of

Lynne. In fact, it seemed like the bond between mother and daughter for those three days may have bolstered Lynne's spirits and improved her overall condition. Sadly, things would change shortly thereafter.

There was a running argument between Hospice and the Senior Home Care service about restraints. True restraints – like tying down a patients legs or arms in bed - violated Hospice rules, based on the presumption that they caused pain that infringed upon the principle of comfort care. We never used those kinds of restraints but we did fashion an old blanket that we wrapped around Lynne's ~~waste,~~ waist tying it behind her chair. As she spent a considerable amount of her time trying to get up out of that chair, she would have fallen repeatedly without it. So we kept ~~in all~~ it on at all times but quickly slipped it off when the Hospice team arrived.

After being in home hospice for about a month, Lynne was still not sleeping through the night – raising havoc with our own sleep schedules. Our main Hospice nurse recommended transfer to the hospital's satellite inpatient Hospice unit for three or four days – so the medical team could observe her sleep behavior and adjust her medications. The inpatient unit was a very pretty building in a bucolic setting about fifteen miles from our home. I reluctantly agreed to the transfer, but Lynne – despite all of our reassurances about the temporary nature of this "admission", was convinced that we were transferring her to a permanent nursing home and resisted the whole idea. The facility had a large, central, wide-open living area overlooking a beautiful lake. Lynne fell out of bed during her first night there. Again no major injuries but I was hoping that the inpatient team would provide more constant observations. We had become accustomed to someone either sitting or sleeping with Lynne 24/7 at home. The medical team decided to switch her from Seroquel to Depakote for sleep, but it was going to take three days to get the new drug delivered to the facility.

One of my worst memories of Lynne's entire ordeal occurred when I visited her on the second day of her stay at the inpatient Hospice facility. When I arrived she was sitting alone in the large living area. There was a plate of food sitting in front of her and she appeared very peaceful looking at the snow falling on the lake outside the window. When I walked up to her to give her a kiss and a hug she started balling her eyes out. I hadn't seen that kind of emotional reaction from her for many months. When I asked why she was crying she looked me in the eyes and said, "I didn't think I would ever see you again." Once again, she was convinced that I had put her in a permanent nursing home and left her there to die. The sad look on her face broke my heart.

It turns out that the inpatient Hospice facility was also referred to as a "Respite Center". I was told that in any given quarter, I could have Lynne transferred to the Center for up to five days – either consecutively or broken up to as little as one day at a time – in order to give me and the family respite from the daily grind of taking care of her. It sounded great, but after seeing Lynne sobbing with thoughts of abandonment, I secretly promised myself that I would never voluntarily bring her back to the Center. Taking care of her was difficult but I wanted her to be in our home – even if she thought she was somewhere else!

The nurses and other professionals at the Respite Center were extremely pleasant, professional, and caring – much like all of the members of the Hospice team. However, the experience for Lynne was not the positive one that we had hoped for. I insisted on taking Lynne home after the third night in the Center. I reasoned that, being a physician, I could make the recommended adjustments of her medications and discuss any changes by telephone with the Hospice team. I was waiting at home when an ambulance moved her from the Respite Center back to our house. The smile on Lynne's face as she re-entered our home made the entire inpatient ordeal worthwhile. She *did* recognize her home after all – at least transiently.

Although I got plenty of help from my children, there were many hours during the week when it was just me and Lynne in the house. During that time I often said I felt like a single parent caring for a newborn. When Lynne cried out, "Mom, Dad, Judy" or other names that I never before heard of – it usually meant she was wet, soiled, hungry, or just needed a change of position. Before her medications were changed after her stay in inpatient hospice center, Lynne was also like a newborn in that she would wake up as often as once an hour – sometimes needing a diaper change, but often just exhibiting free-floating agitation and anxiety.

I finally came up with a cocktail of medications that got Lynne to sleep throughout the night: One milligram of lorezapam at 5 pm. At 8 pm I'd give her an additional one milligram of lorezapam together with two hundred and fifty milligrams of Depakote. This was all based on bedtime being 8:30 pm. After moving her into bed I would give her one milligram of oral morphine sulfate and kept an additional half a milligram of the morphine at the bedside in case she woke up in the middle of the night. All of this was in addition to the Depakote. With this regimen she slept from 8:30 pm till at least 7 am most nights – and occasionally she slept until 10 am.

However, she would still occasionally wake up in the middle of the night to bother her companion. Lauren tells the story about one night when she told Lynne that "It was time for bed. Have sweet dreams." Two hours later, Lynne awoke, tapped Lauren on the shoulder and said "I don't know what to dream about." Lauren replied, "Dream about how much you love your family." Lynne rolled over and slept soundly for the remainder of the night.

When I had the "cot duty" and was convinced she was sleeping I would often stay awake for another hour or two, sitting in the *old* family room, watching some silly show on the Food Network channel, and meditating. I eventually moved back to the *new* family room to sleep on the cot next to Lynne's bed, but often had difficulty falling sleep. A glass of wine and fifty milligrams of Benadryl usually helped.

Chapter 13

Last Days

For those first few months of home hospice, I often found myself asking 'How will this all end?' After all, Lynne was not a cancer patient given only a few weeks to live. "How do patients with dementia die?" The most common answer I got from Hospice team proved to be partly true: 'They stop eating and eventually die from starvation'.

Lynne had been eating surprisingly well until about a month before her death. Then she developed some difficulty swallowing foods and experienced several bouts of choking – even on soft foods like scrambled eggs that she previously swallowed without a problem. I could only guess that the muscles required to swallow food had atrophied like her other muscles. We resorted to giving her only pureed foods, but this markedly reduced her caloric intake and a vicious cycle ensued: less eating, more weight loss and weakness, further difficulties with swallowing. I started giving her some liquids and protein powder concoctions through her gastrostomy tube, but it was hard to get more than five hundred calories a day into her. Furthermore I knew I was violating our initial promise to avoid tube feedings. I could see the end coming and felt desperate. Around this time we noted a dark purplish discoloration of Lynne's feet – especially noticeable when she had been sitting up for a prolonged period of time, but even present to some extent when she was lying in bed. To me, it had the appearance of venous insufficiency but there was no good reason for her to have problems with her circulation. Our main Hospice nurse told us that she had seen this kind of discoloration many times in pre-terminal patients with dementia. Together with the difficulty swallowing and the inevitable malnutrition, she noted that these signs often heralded the "beginning of the end." And of course she was right.

Throughout this entire ordeal, family and friends often advised me to take off some time to rest and relax and to take my mind off of caring for Lynne. Admittedly, the short trip to New York in April provided a much needed, albeit small dose of rejuvenation. Two years earlier, we bought a vacation home in the Outer Banks of North Carolina. It was mostly a rental property but my family stayed at the home for one week in the spring and one week in the fall. Lynne actually made the trip with us in May of 2017 (the last time she flew with me anywhere) and, although she was unable to do much more than sit on a couch or on the outdoor porch overlooking Roanoke Sound. Lynne always loved being on or near a body of water, finding it spiritually uplifting.

I booked the home for the first week of May 2018. I knew Lynne could no longer make the trip, but the plan was for me to go for three days, joining my sons and two friends for a trip that would include deep-sea fishing for tuna and mahi-mahi. My sons drove down with their friends one day before I planned to fly down via Norfolk, Virginia. My daughter, Lauren, would once again stay behind to be with Lynne.

On the day my sons left for North Carolina (about a twelve hour drive), Lynne started vomiting. She had previous episodes of choking, but vomiting was not a common problem for her since entering hospice. I had been using her gastrostomy tube regularly for some liquid food intake and for administering medications, but now, for the first time, whenever I injected something into the tube, Lynne would immediately vomit suggesting that she had free reflux from her stomach back up her esophagus.

I knew if she didn't improve, I might have to cancel my trip to the Outer Banks. I had a 7:30 am flight the next morning, which meant that I would have to leave for the airport by 5:30 am. Lauren slept on the cot next to Lynne that night. However, Lynne woke up at 3 am and had intractable vomiting. Lauren knocked on the door of my upstairs bedroom and told me she needed help. I gave Lynne an additional 1 mg of morphine. It was in a liquid form that presumably was absorbed from the mouth so that it didn't need to be swallowed. I replaced Lauren on the cot and asked her to get

51

some sleep on the couch in the old family room. After thirty minutes Lynne fell asleep and appeared to stabilize.

Do I go to North Carolina or not? At 5 am I got the brilliant idea of going online and changing my flight from 7:30 am to a 2:30 pm flight through Newark. I would arrive in North Carolina late but would still be there for the fishing excursion the next day. This plan would give me another half day to be sure that Lynne was stable. Maybe she just had a twenty-four hour bug. I made all of the arrangements online and hopped back onto the cot at 6 am. At 6:30 am, Lynne woke up with projectile vomiting – mostly green bile colored stuff. Lauren woke up to help. My biggest fear was aspiration, so we sat Lynne bolt upright as she filled one basin after another with green liquid.

There was no way I could go to North Carolina. I notified my sons by text messages, trying not to alarm them about Lynne's deterioration. About six hours later, I received text messages from United Airlines announcing that my flights from Cleveland to Newark and Newark to Norfolk were both cancelled due to air traffic control problems. *Someone* was making sure I did not leave home.

Lynne's vomiting subsided, mostly because her oral intake fell to zero in the next two days. I stopped using the gastrostomy tube because even small infusions caused her to regurgitate. Even sips of water or clear liquids led to choking.

On Saturday May 5, a Senior Care aid stayed overnight with Lynne so I could get some sleep in my own bedroom. The aid woke me up at 4 am saying "Lynne doesn't look too good. She's not breathing well". When I got downstairs I immediately recognized agonal respirations. Lynne was gurgling (sometimes referred to as a 'death rattle'). She had almost certainly aspirated – another common mode of death for hospice patients. I let the aid go home for the rest of the night and laid on the cot next to Lynne, getting up every fifteen minutes to be sure she was breathing. At 7:30 am I called Lauren who was staying at her own home about two miles away, and told her that her Mom's breathing was erratic. She joined me fifteen minutes later, promptly greeted by her mother with a prolonged bout of vomiting that soiled all of her bed clothes and sheets. Lauren cleaned up the mess. She worked in the Oncology Division at the hospital and had lots of experience dealing with death in cancer patients. She agreed that her mother's breathing appeared *agonal* and that Lynne was dying. We both noticed that the clamped tube hanging from her gastrostomy site was filled with dark brown coffee ground-like material, almost certainly reflecting some pre-terminal bleeding from the stomach.

My two sons were returning from North Carolina that morning and had already texted me to tell me they took off at 6 am. I was reluctant to call them for fear they would freak out and cause an accident on the road. I did call our son, Kevin, in Chicago, and told him to make plans to head home as soon as possible.

Lynne's breathing became shallow. She never appeared to be in any pain. Lauren said, "I love you Mom", and Lynne responded, "I love you too". I asked my wife, "Do you know who I am?" and she responded, "Doctor Don" – her last words. Kevin was on the phone and Lauren had turned on the speaker mode. As Kevin was telling his mother how much he loved her, she took her last gasp and passed away. She died as her "miracle child" was thanking her for everything she had done for him in his lifetime. I will never forget holding Lynne's hand and watching her take her last breath. The image regularly haunts me, partly because it reminds me of my own mortality and the mortality of the people who live around me.

For days, weeks and even years after a loved one dies, we all like to recall the notable "lasts" – last visits, last words, last baths. Lauren reminded me that, the day before she died, Lynne watched her favorite Jack Nicholson movie – a movie that she had watched dozens of times before – one *last* time. Some of these milestones are more memorable than others. But I will never, ever forget that last look on Lynne's face – eyes open, staring beyond me and Lauren, beyond the last vestiges of her life on Earth. Although it is a sad image and memory, I'll forever be truthful and happy in saying that Lynne looked to be at peace. She died *peacefully.*

I called the Hospice nurse on-call as I had been instructed to do all along in the case of death. She arrived promptly to prepare the body for delivery to the funeral home. Hearing about our family situation, she urged to me call my sons on the road rather than to have them walk in nine hours later to find out their mother had died hours earlier. She then offered a thought that was profoundly insightful. "You know Don, she planned on dying today with all of the boys – including you – out of town. As a mother, she knew there would be less drama if it were just she with her daughter. It's so nice that both you and Lauren could be here as she passed away, but I've been in this business a long time and I'm telling you – Mothers want to cause as little pain to their children as possible. Mothers know."

Chapter 14

Grieving

I don't think my children and I fully appreciated the physical and mental fatigue that consumed us during those home hospice days until Lynne finally passed away. Those nights sleeping on the couch next to Lynne were particularly laborious and I think we all suffered from sleep deprivation. When Lynne died, there was sadness of course, but also a sense of incredible relief – not only the relief that Lynne was finally free of pain, but some selfish relief that we could finally relax and get back to leading normal lives. I promised myself then and now, that I would try to make life as normal as possible for my children after Lynne passed away. It has not been an easy chore. It was both a blessing and a curse that my retirement date virtually coincided with Lynne's death. It gave me more free time to spend with my children but also more time to reflect on Lynne's illness and passing.

Lynne died at the age of sixty-four – awfully young for someone to develop severe and fatal dementia. I wrote down these memories of my wife within two weeks of her death – mostly so I would not forget them and could read them again and again - and never forget. Almost all of us have had to deal with death of a loved one and the subsequent grieving. So I am not making the case that my loss is any worse than others have experienced. However, I do hope that my memories of Lynne and my family's ordeal with her illness will provide some solace to others who have cared for loved ones with dementia.

We were fortunate to have Father Tom Fanta preside over Lynne's funeral service. I miss Lynne tremendously and will always miss her, but hearing and re-reading Father Tom's homily (see the epilogue below) has eased the pain.

EPILOGUE

Father Tom's Funeral Homily for Lynne

I grew up not too far from here in North Olmsted...and as a kid...I attended St. Brendan Church. I remember growing up going to Catholic Schools...and from the very beginning teachers telling us that Mary, the mother of Jesus, was the model Christian, and that we should always strive to be just like her. And I remember clearly in the church I grew up in there was a large statue of the Blessed Mother right next to the altar....and like a lot of statues of Mary...she stood there with her eyes downcast and her hands folded...and I would sit there as a little kid...bored at mass...and I would look up at that statue and think..."She looks boring...why would I want to be like her?"

And so I must have been in about the second or third grade, and my grandpa just a few streets away decided to build a little shrine to Mary in his backyard. And so we dug a hole and poured cement and my grandpa made a brick foundation and then one of those little wooden houses...and all the while I was thinking why would he want that sad statue in the backyard? And so we finally finished and we went into the garage to get the box with the new statue.

And my grandpa carefully took out all of the Styrofoam and packaging and then hold up this statue...but it wasn't like the one at Church...no, this statue was of Mary with her hands extended and a smile on her face. And I remember thinking..."Now that is a Mary I can relate to. That is a Mary that I want to be like. That is a Mary who has a real faith.....a smile on her face...with hands extended out to others in service...joyfully living her faith.

When I think about Lynne...that is the image that comes to mind...a beautiful woman who lived her life with her hands extended to others...a beautiful smile on her face...joyfully living her faith.

In our gospel this morning, Jesus proclaims..."Do not let your hearts be troubled. Trust in me. For I am the way and the truth and the life."

Yet those are hard words to hear...how can our hearts not be troubled?

How does this family go on without their mom, their grandma, their wife?

Why did this happen?

Why do we have to feel this way?

Why couldn't there be a cure for Lynne?

And I really don't have the answers to those questions. I don't know why she had to leave us so young...but I do know, I do know that Lynne knew the way...she knew the way and the truth and the life of Jesus...and with her hands extended out to us..and that beautiful smile on her face...she tried to lead all of us along the way. Her friends and neighbors knew the way of Jesus through Lynne's life. Her pool parties on High Parkway were legendary...and the meals she prepared for guests were unmatched. I have known her for 25 years...and throughout all of those years she was always the first to share good news...whether in the grocery store..a neighborhood restaurant...or just walking down the street...Lynne always had an encouraging word, a quick laugh...a beautiful smile on her face. You just felt good when you were around her...and each time you went to her home...she made you feel special...she made you feel welcome. There was always room for one more at her table...and she always just seemed to radiate joy...reminding you of the goodness of people...she was a blessing to so many people.

Her family surely knew the way of Jesus in her life...because for Lynne...her children and grandchild were her life. They were her vocation. They were her reason for living. I became very close to Lynne many years ago when Kevin was sick....and I remember countless visits with her and Kevin at the hospital. And no matter how hopeless it seemed...no matter how bad a day Kevin had....Lynne kept believing...she kept trusting...she was so convinced that God would help her son to live. When so many others had given up hope....Lynne's faith..her hands outstretched in prayer...her positive outlook...I will never forget the faith she taught me.

Over those years I watched her with Brian and Lauren and Michael....and each one of you...her 4 beautiful treasures...her passion in life. Each of you had your own distinct relationship with her.

Brian...with his beautiful daughter Brielle...who was the joy of Lynne's life. Brielle...you were her dolly wolly...and she loved every time you came to visit. She was there for you Brian in your darkest hours...and you were there for her in her dark times as well.

And Lauren...she was so proud of the woman you have become. Your wisdom...your laughter...your beauty. You are so much like your mom...always bringing joy to others.

And of course Kevin...Lynne's own private miracle....every conversation I had with her over these many years always included a story about Kevin and the wonderful man you have become.

And Michael...her baby...who I think was born with a smile on his face...whose gentleness and kindness are just a perfect reflection of his mom.

I have watched in these last years as your mom got sicker....your fear...your confusion...your sadness. Your mom is the heart of your family...and she will always be that heart. I once read that "A mother's love will follow you wherever you go." But I think for all of you...your mother's love will lead you wherever you go. Pray to your mom...ask her to help you. Listen for her voice to guide you. Keep her at the heart of every family gathering. Remember all the values she taught you...I don't have to tell you how much your mom loved you...because she told you all the time. God gave you a special gift in your mom...a gift you will always have in your lives. Remember her example of holiness...remember her faith...and follow her example..with your hands outstretched to others...revealing God's love in all that you say and do.

And finally....Don....40 years ago you stood at an altar and made promises to Lynne...and you said that you would be true to her in good times and in bad...in sickness and in health...you said you would love her and honor her all the days of your life. And you did just that. You had a true love affair...with a love that was so very clear to all of us. She supported you in all that you have accomplished in your career..yet you always just seemed to marvel at all she had done in her career as the mother of your children. Your mutual respect...your travels together...your quiet nights in the backyard...you were everything to her...and she was everything to you. Your marriage was a gift...and the love you shared does not disappear with the passing of her earthly body.

Continue to talk with her..argue with her..laugh with her and cry with her. You have a lifetime of memories of her love...use those memories to sustain you in the days ahead.

It was just a few months ago that I last saw Lynne. She was at University Hospitals and she was struggling so much....and I walked into her room...and she was sitting up in her bed looking out the window. And as I came toward her she extended both of her hands...and as sick as she was...she still had that beautiful smile on her face. And we prayed together and I anointed her with oil...and we talked about her frustration and her fear....and about the beautiful life that God had given her. And as I left the hospital that day...I just said a prayer of thanks to God for this beautiful friend who taught me so much about faith and trust and families.

Lynne was truly a blessed mother. She was a blessed wife and a blessed friend. And perhaps the best way for all of us to give thanks to God for her life would be to leave this place with our hands extended to others and a smile on our faces...and continue to follow the way...follow the way and the truth and the life of Jesus. So that one day we might see Lynne again and enjoy her love to the fullest.

Other Books by Donald Hricik

Racing to Pittsburgh

Nothing to Confess

Escape from Cleveland

Our Great Escape; Part 1: Dumbers

Coming Soon

Our Great Escape; Part 2: Return to the Tunnel People

Made in the USA
Lexington, KY
08 December 2018